VAST — THE DRAMA OF AUSTRALIAN LANDSCAPES

Steve Parish

Vast

The Drama of Australian Landscapes

Vast

I have travelled the length and breadth of this expansive continent many times and each time I have been captivated by the grandeur of its vast landscapes. Many people are unable to fully experience the immensity of this land, so I wanted this book to provide a breathtaking, behind-the-scenes look at Australia, as it is now and as the Aborigines and early Europeans must have seen it.

More than any other photographic subject, landscapes transport the viewer to places they may never have been. I hope this book takes you to the baking red Australian Outback, which stretches for an eternity under a canopy of blue. I hope it takes you on a journey down rivers as they carve ravines through seemingly impenetrable rock, or allows you to absorb for a moment the spirituality of Carnarvon Gorge's rock art galleries or the serenity of beaches sculpted by tide and time. Most of all, I hope it impresses on you the vast, unique beauty of this ancient, time-weathered continent.

Steve Parish

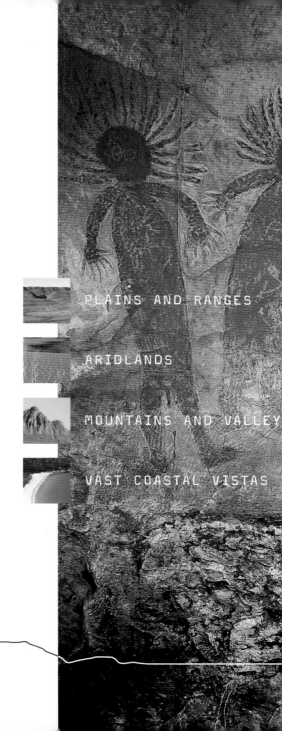

Over hills and over plains,

Quiet, vast and slumbrous, reigns.

(Charles Harpur, 1813-1868)

Plains and Randes

Breezes whisper through the spindly branches of pandanus trees at Fogg Dam Conservation Reserve, Northern Territory.

Boabs stand as sentinels in Keep River National Park, Northern Territory.

Trees, stretching skywards, are silent *guardians* of the plains' ancient secrets...

Jim Jim Falls in full flood following the wet season,
Kakadu National Park, Northern Territory.

The rocky lookout at Ubirr provides a spectacular vista of the Nardab floodplains, Kakadu National Park, Northern Territory.

From the black hills that loomed around

The valley many a sudden *spire*

Of flame shot up...

(Victor Daley, 1858–1905)

Colossal sandstone pillars form a protective citadel above a tract of monsoonal rainforest, Nathan River, Northern Territory.

Mysterious tiger-striped strata of the Bungle Bungle Range, Purnululu National Park, Western Australia.

Two timeless forces in nature converge at Katherine Gorge, Nitmiluk National Park, Northern Territory.

The Katherine River winds through the Arnhem Land plateau, Nitmiluk National Park, Northern Territory.

Rivers *cleave* dramatic gorges through vivid *sandstone*

Stout Boabs squat in the ranges over the Pentecost River, the Kimberley, Western Australia.

Aboriginal rock art depicting Wandjinas, or creation beings, who during the Dreaming brought their world and all its inhabitants into existence, Keep River National Park, Northern Territory.

An *ancient* heart beats in this landscape
of challenging cliff-rimmed *ranges* and fast-flowing rivers.

(Henry Lawson, 1867–1922)

In a country characterised by its remoteness, the Kimberley, Western Australia, represents some of the most isolated landscape in the continent.

Top: Negotiating a path across the Pentecost River Crossing in the Kimberley's north-east, Western Australia, requires steady nerves and intense concentration.
Above: Lennard River Gorge, on the western side of the King Leopold Ranges in Western Australia.

The Endeavour River weaves a sinuous passage through a vast stretch of scrub near Cooktown, Queensland.

Tropical wetlands near Shelburne Bay, Cape York Peninsula, Queensland.

Undara Volcanic National Park, Queensland.

Limestone outcrops are all that remain of an ancient coral reef that once existed near Chillagoe in western Queensland.

If nature stirs you to such pleasure, just think how she must stir me...

discovering the laws that govern the *everlasting*

might and splendour of her workings...

(Ludwig Leichhardt, 1813–1848)

Bands of sunlight illuminate the entrance to an underworld of lava tubes in Undara Volcanic National Park, Queensland.

Those who lose *dreaming* are lost.

(*Aboriginal proverb*)

About 190,000 years ago, a violent eruption covered the landscape of Undara Volcanic National Park. While the surface lava cooled to a crust, the molten magma within continued to drain away, like hot water inside a pipe, leaving behind a series of hollow tubes which form the largest cave system of its kind on Earth.

Canoeists savour the lush sanctuary of Lawn Hill Gorge, Queensland.

Aridlands

Nothing could exceed the desolation around us.

Not a herb or flower was to be seen

but the land was perfectly bare and scorched...

(Charles Sturt, 1795-1869)

Dazzling rays of sun clash with the rugged angles of sandstone in the Rainbow Valley Conservation Reserve, Northern Territory.

The Painted Desert, South Australia, is an enigmatic wilderness of natural contrasts.

The sublime minimalism of the Painted Desert, South Australia.

A lone gum becomes a singular, stoic apparition at the foot of the Flinders Ranges, South Australia.

Despite its inhospitable appearance, the rugged country around Flinders Range National Park sustained the Adnyamathanha Indigenous tribes over thousands of years.

Aboriginal artwork tells the stories of their culture.

Trees punctuating the landscape of Flinders Ranges National Park do little to interrupt the sense of space and solitude.

Out on the *wastes* of the Never Never...

There where the heat-waves dance for ever...

(Barcroft Boake, 1866–1892)

A settler's lonely grave, South Australia, is a poignant reminder of the unrelenting nature of Terra Australis.

The sun beats upon Australia's aridlands with a merciless amplitude.

The Australian Outback surrenders its horizon to desolation on the gibber plains of Queensland.

Top: An iron-grey sky boils on the horizon over channel country – a massive and labyrinthine drainage system on the remote plains of Queensland's south-west.
Above: Moonda Lake, part of a lake system between Birdsville and Betoota, Queensland.

Skies smoulder with the sudden squalls and *rains*
that bring life to wetlands and *replenish* billabongs.

Trees drenched in the ephemeral bronze of sunset, New South Wales.

No other image evokes the spirituality of the Australian landscape more than Uluru in the Northern Territory.

The rugged elegance of the Flinders Ranges, South Australia.

Ancient red desert bakes beneath an overarching dome of brilliant blue.

Dry *deserts* with long pent up passion.

(Adam Lindsay Gordon, 1833–1870)

Burt Bluff, in the heartland of the Red Centre, western MacDonnell Ranges, Northern Territory.

The MacDonnell Ranges extend over 150 kilometres, stretching west from Alice Springs in a series of spectacular parallel ridges.

New Holland is a very *large* tract of land...

(William Dampier, 1652–1715)

Karijini National Park, Western Australia.

The soft, twilight hues of the Outback bestow calm on the Hamersley Range, Karijini National Park, Western Australia.

A blanket of wildflowers brighten the red plains surrounding the world's largest monolith, Mt Augustus, Western Australia.

Nature has enough *space* to free the spirit within us all...

Wide open plains spread before Mt Augustus.

Where the pine-clad ridges raise

Their torn and rugged battlements on high...

(Banjo Paterson, 1864-1941)

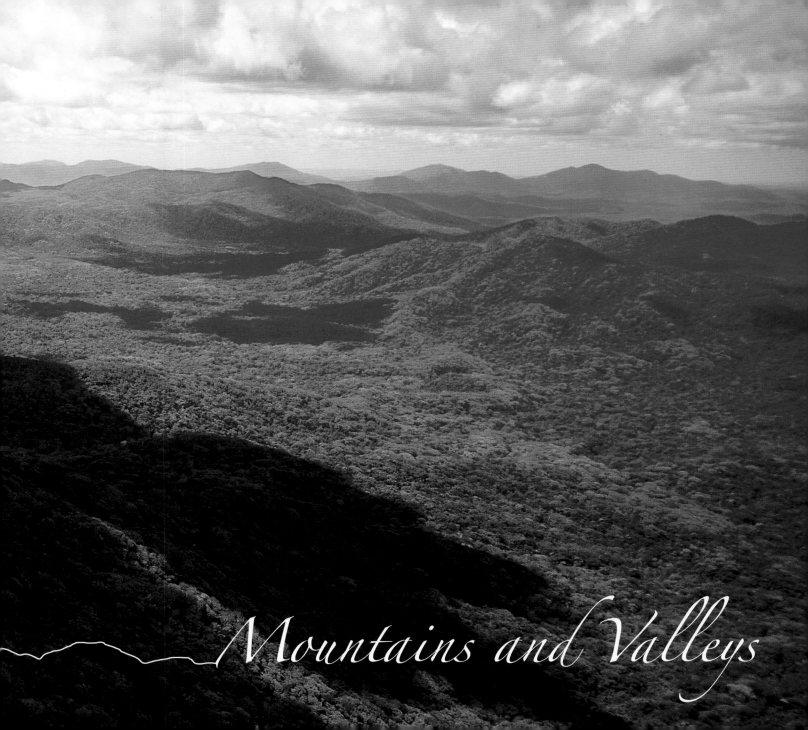

Mountains and Valleys

Johnstone River gliding beneath the rainforest's overhanging bower, Wooroonooran National Park, Queensland.

Cool, rushing cascades in the Mossman River, Daintree National Park, Queensland.

...the tall gum-trees, among which I first saw the *light*, are real

in their stateliness and substantiality...

(Miles Franklin, 1879–1954)

Prehistoric sandstone cliffs beyond tall Cabbage Tree Palms at Carnarvon Gorge, Queensland.

An extensive collection of fragile rock art – including stencils, engravings and freehand paintings – decorates the cliffs and caves of Carnarvon Gorge, Queensland.

Carnarvon Gorge, an oasis in the central Queensland Outback.

Open and spacious eucalypt forests are just one of a multitude of diverse environments within the Bunya Mountains, Queensland.

Cunninghams Gap, the monumental pass over the Great Dividing Range between Brisbane and the Darling Downs, Main Range National Park, Queensland.

Mt Maroon, part of the ruggedly spectacular Scenic Rim, Mt Barney National Park, Queensland.

A thousand echoes rang

And died away among the *hills* ...

(Barcroft Boake, 1866–1892)

Undulating golden grasslands span the low plains before Mt Barney, Mt Barney National Park, Queensland.

There are few things more pleasing than the *contemplation* of order and useful arrangement.

(Govenor Arthur Phillip, 1738–1814)

Above and right: Razor-like crags breach the forested ridges of the Warrumbungles, New South Wales.

The famous triumvirate of sandstone siblings, the Three Sisters, perched atop a gulf of cloud overseeing the Jamison Valley, Blue Mountains National Park, New South Wales.

Not a sound disturbs the air, There is *quiet* everywhere...

(Charles Harpur, 1813–1868)

Peering into the disquieting mist shrouding Perry's Lookdown, Blue Mountains National Park, New South Wales.

Mornings in the Blue Mountains are a transcendental experience.

Alpine landscape in Kosciuszko National Park, New South Wales.

The moon fades in a dazzling clear sky as dawn awakens Mt Kosciuszko.

The immense breadth of the Australian landscape extends into all environments, Mt Hotham, Victorian Alps.

A lurid sunset paints the sky beyond Mt Buffalo, Victoria.

A distant *horizon* gives us more than perspective.
It dares us to dream.

Grampians, Victoria.

Mt William is typical of the mountainous splendour on display in the Grampians.

The vaulted dolerite summit of Cradle Mountain looms over Dove Lake in Cradle Mountain–Lake St Clair National Park, a Tasmanian Wilderness World Heritage Area.

A storm breaks into a rainbow over the Arthur Range, Southwest National Park, Tasmania.

And in the air a little wind that tells

Of moonlit waves beyond a murmuring surf...

(J.A.R Mackellar, 1904-1932)

Vast Coastal Vistas

Snow-dusted Mt Wellington presides over the city of Hobart and the mouth of the Derwent River, Tasmania.

The pristine majesty of Wineglass Bay, Freycinet National Park, Tasmania.

Above: The imposing grandeur of Precipitous Bluff, viewed from Prion Bay on the south coast of Southwest National Park, Tasmania.
Right: Rocks jut out into the ocean landscape in Southwest National Park, Tasmania.

Ambition leads me not only *farther* than any other man has been before me, but as far as I think it's possible for man to go.

(James Cook, 1728–1799)

The lighthouse at Victoria's Southern Ocean outpost, Wilsons Promontory, warns vessels navigating the treacherous seas of Bass Strait.

Top: Forged by the relentless wash of the sea, the Twelve Apostles form an iconic image, Port Campbell National Park, Victoria.
Bottom: Little Penguins march home over the sands following a day's fishing.

Australia is properly speaking an *island*, but it is so much larger than every other island on the face of the globe, that it is classed as a continent in order to convey to the mind a just idea of its *magnitude*

(Charles Sturt, 1795–1869)

Intrepid hikers perched atop Mt Oberon, on Wilsons Promontory, Victoria, are rewarded with stunning views over Bass Strait.

Cape du Couedic Lighthouse is a prominent landmark of Kangaroo Island, Flinders Chase National Park, South Australia.

...who should examine into the natural productions of this *wonderful* country, for surely what has been found is materially different from all others...

(Matthew Flinders, 1774–1814)

Brick-orange lichen emblazen the Remarkable Rocks, Flinders Chase National Park, South Australia.

Coffin Bay National Park, on the edge of the Great Australian Bight, is a desolate and beautiful expanse of South Australian coastline.

It is ironic that the coastal hills of Fitzgerald River National Park, Western Australia, are known as The Barrens because the area is home to more than 1800 plant species.

We must endure humility in the presence of a stone's *eternal* time.

Waves surge beneath the massive stone arch of Natural bridge, Torndirrup National Park, Tasmania.

An aerial view of Torndirrup National Park, Tasmania, featuring Bald Head, the Salmon Holes and Isthmus Bay.

The great, vermilion wall of Zuytdorp Cliffs, Western Australia, rises to 170 metres above the ocean, yet in 1712 a few desperate survivors of the Dutch ship *Zuytdorp* somehow managed to ascend the sheer cliffs.

The spectacular span of the Zuytdorp Cliffs.

Furnace-red desert plains ignite the beaches of Shark Bay with stunning contrasts, François Peron National Park, Western Australia.

Saltwater and the ravages of time have sculpted these rocks at Roebuck Bay, Western Australia.

In these hours when life is *ebbing*, how those days when life was young   Come back to us...

(Adam Lindsay Gordon, 1833–1870)

The striated headland of Gantheaume Point, just south-west of Broome, Western Australia, is caressed by the turquoise tides of Gantheaume Bay.

Beaches around Darwin in the Northern Territory are fringed with eucalypt scrub, mangroves and tidal outcrops.

Sunset magic envelops the tropics, Darwin.

A grand panorama of the Endeavour River and the hinterland viewed from Grassy Hill, Cooktown, Queensland.

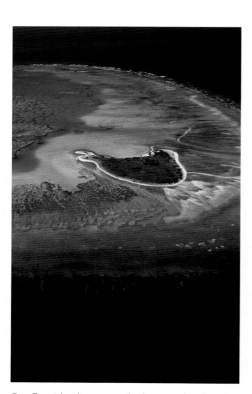

One Tree Island, an untouched National Park in the centre of the Capricorn Group, Great Barrier Reef.

The Great Barrier Reef, stretching along the central to north Queensland coast, is one of the greatest wonders of the natural world.

Whitehaven Beach, Hill Inlet and Tongue Point adorn unspoilt Whitsunday Island, Queensland.

Mountainous white dunes are an extraordinary spectacle on Queensland's World-Heritage-listed Fraser Island, the largest sand island on Earth.

The stretching foreshore of Main Beach invites relaxed introspection, North Stradbroke Island, Queensland.

Above: Cape Byron Lighthouse, New South Wales, grants tourists Australia's easternmost vantage point for observing the great cobalt void of the Pacific.
Left: Surfers share a serene dusk over the hinterland of Byron Bay, New South Wales.

We are all visitors to this time, this place.

We are just *passing* through. Our purpose here is to observe, to learn,

to grow, to love... and then to return home.

(Aboriginal proverb)

online

FOR PRODUCTS
www.steveparish.com.au

FOR LIMITED EDITION PRINTS
www.steveparishexhibits.com.au

FOR PHOTOGRAPHY EZINE
www.photographaustralia.com.au

© copyright Steve Parish Publishing Pty Ltd
PO Box 1058, Archerfield, Queensland 4108 Australia
ISBN 174021928 7
10 9 8 7 6 5 4 3 2 1

Photography: Steve Parish

Text: Ted Lewis, SPP

Design: Leanne Nobilio, SPP

Editing: Karin Cox, SPP

Acknowledgements:
The publishers are grateful for permission to reproduce
copyright material. Whilst every effort has been made
to trace copyright holders, the publisher would be
pleased to hear from any not here acknowledged.

Front cover & title page: Flinders Ranges, South Australia. Pages 2–3,
left to right: Hummock Grass on a stony plain in central Queensland;
Aboriginal rock art, Keep River National Park, Northern Territory. Pages
6–7 Boab trees in the Kimberley, Western Australia. Pages 28–29:
Simpson Desert, Northern Territory. Pages 56–57: Thornton Peak,
Daintree National Park, Queensland. Pages 96–97: Anthony Beach,
Perkins Bay, north-west Tasmania.

Printed in China by PrintPlus Ltd

Pre-press by Colour Chiefs Digital Imaging, Brisbane, Australia

Produced in Australia at the Steve Parish Publishing Studios